C000218905

by Iain Gray

LangSyne

PUBLISHING

WRITING *to* REMEMBER

LangSyne
PUBLISHING
WRITING *to* REMEMBER

79 Main Street, Newtongrange,
Midlothian EH22 4NA
Tel: 0131 344 0414   Fax: 0845 075 6085
E-mail: info@lang-syne.co.uk
www.langsyneshop.co.uk

Design by Dorothy Meikle
Printed by Printwell Ltd
© Lang Syne Publishers Ltd 2017

ISBN 978-1-85217-536-8

Davies

MOTTO:
Without God without anything,
God is enough.

CREST:
The head of a lion
(and)
The head of a boar.

NAME variations include:
Dakin
Daves
Davis
Davidson
Divis
Dawson
Day

Chapter one:

The origins of popular surnames

by George Forbes and Iain Gray

If you don't know where you came from, you won't know where you're going is a frequently quoted observation and one that has a particular resonance today when there has been a marked upsurge in interest in genealogy, with increasing numbers of people curious to trace their family roots.

Main sources for genealogical research include census returns and official records of births, marriages and deaths – and the key to unlocking the detail they contain is obviously a family surname, one that has been 'inherited' and passed from generation to generation.

No matter our station in life, we all have a surname – but it was not until about the middle of the fourteenth century that the practice of being identified by a particular surname became commonly established throughout the British Isles.

Previous to this, it was normal for a person to be identified through the use of only a forename.

But as population gradually increased and there were many more people with the same forename, surnames were adopted to distinguish one person, or community, from another.

Many common English surnames are patronymic in origin, meaning they stem from the forename of one's father – with 'Johnson,' for example, indicating 'son of John.'

It was the Normans, in the wake of their eleventh century conquest of Anglo-Saxon England, a pivotal moment in the nation's history, who first brought surnames into usage – although it was a gradual process.

For the Normans, these were names initially based on the title of their estates, local villages and chateaux in France to distinguish and identify these landholdings.

Such grand descriptions also helped enhance the prestige of these warlords and generally glorify their lofty positions high above the humble serfs slaving away below in the pecking order who had only single names, often with Biblical connotations as in Pierre and Jacques.

The only descriptive distinctions among the peasantry concerned their occupations, like 'Pierre the swineherd' or 'Jacques the ferryman.'

Roots of surnames that came into usage in England not only included Norman-French, but also Old French, Old Norse, Old English, Middle English, German, Latin, Greek, Hebrew and the Gaelic languages of the Celts.

The Normans themselves were originally Vikings, or 'Northmen', who raided, colonised and eventually settled down around the French coastline.

The had sailed up the Seine in their longboats in 900AD under their ferocious leader Rollo and ruled the roost in north eastern France before sailing over to conquer England in 1066 under Duke William of Normandy – better known to posterity as William the Conqueror, or King William I of England.

Granted lands in the newly-conquered England, some of their descendants later acquired territories in Wales, Scotland and Ireland – taking not only their own surnames, but also the practice of adopting a surname, with them.

But it was in England where Norman rule and custom first impacted, particularly in relation to the adoption of surnames.

This is reflected in the famous *Domesday Book*, a massive survey of much of England and Wales, ordered by William I, to determine who owned what, what it was worth and therefore how much they were liable to pay in taxes to the voracious Royal Exchequer.

Completed in 1086 and now held in the National Archives in Kew, London, 'Domesday' was an Old English word meaning 'Day of Judgement.'

This was because, in the words of one contemporary chronicler, "its decisions, like those of the Last Judgement, are unalterable."

It had been a requirement of all those English landholders – from the richest to the poorest – that they identify themselves for the purposes of the survey and for future reference by means of a surname.

This is why the *Domesday Book*, although written in Latin as was the practice for several centuries with both civic and ecclesiastical records, is an invaluable source for the early appearance of a wide range of English surnames.

Several of these names were coined in connection with occupations.

These include Baker and Smith, while Cooks, Chamberlains, Constables and Porters were to be found carrying out duties in large medieval households.

The church's influence can be found in names such as Bishop, Friar and Monk while the popular name of Bennett derives from the late fifth to mid-sixth century Saint Benedict, founder of the Benedictine order of monks.

The early medical profession is represented by Barber, while businessmen produced names that include Merchant and Sellers.

Down at the village watermill, the names that cropped up included Millar/Miller, Walker and Fuller, while other self-explanatory trades included Cooper, Tailor, Mason and Wright.

Even the scenery was utilised as in Moor, Hill, Wood and Forrest – while the hunt and the chase supplied names that include Hunter, Falconer, Fowler and Fox.

Colours are also a source of popular surnames, as in Black, Brown, Gray/Grey, Green and White, and would have denoted the colour of the clothing the person habitually wore or, apart from the obvious exception of 'Green', one's hair colouring or even complexion.

The surname Red developed into Reid, while

Blue was rare and no-one wanted to be associated with yellow.

Rather self-important individuals took surnames that include Goodman and Wiseman, while physical attributes crept into surnames such as Small and Little.

Many families proudly boast the heraldic device known as a Coat of Arms, as featured on our front cover.

The central motif of the Coat of Arms would originally have been what was borne on the shield of a warrior to distinguish himself from others on the battlefield.

Not featured on the Coat of Arms, but high-lighted on page three, is the family motto and related crest – with the latter frequently different from the central motif.

Adding further variety to the rich cultural heritage that is represented by surnames is the appearance in recent times in lists of the 100 most common names found in England of ones that include Khan, Patel and Singh – names that have proud roots in the vast sub-continent of India.

Echoes of a far distant past can still be found in our surnames and they can be borne with pride in commemoration of our forebears.

Chapter two:

Of royal pedigree

**A name of ancient roots, 'Davies' is ranked at
number six in some lists of the 100 most common
surnames found in England, but it is in Wales that
it is particularly prevalent.**

Spelling variations of the name include
'Davis', ranked at number 56 in some lists of the most
common surnames, and whose bearers today have
their own separate and proud history.

Derived from the popular personal name of
David, the Davies name is of Biblical roots, with
'David' meaning 'beloved' and also the name of the
Old Testament David, founder of the Jewish Royal
House of David.

The name also became popularised in
medieval times, particularly in Wales, through
veneration for David, the mid to late sixth century
Welsh bishop who was later canonised as a saint and
adopted as the patron saint of Wales.

With a white dove as his emblem, he was a
renowned preacher and teacher and founded a
number of churches and monastic settlements that

include what is now St David's Cathedral, in Pembrokeshire, on the site of one of the monasteries he founded.

While many bearers of common surnames found in both England and Wales today are of Anglo-Saxon roots, bearers of the Davies name are of even earlier Brythonic, or British, origin.

Of Celtic pedigree, these early inhabitants of the British Isles were settled for centuries from a line south of the River Forth in Scotland all the way down to the south coast of England and with a particular presence in Wales.

Speaking a Celtic language known as Brythonic, they boasted a glorious culture that flourished even after the Roman invasion of Britain in 43 AD and the subsequent consolidation of Roman power by about 84 AD.

With many of the original Britons absorbing aspects of Roman culture, they became 'Romano-British' – while still retaining their own proud Celtic heritage.

In a much later century, Edward Davies, born in 1756 in Llanfaredd, Radnorshire, and known as Edward "Celtic" Davies, played an important role in the study of Celtic languages and mythology.

An Anglican clergyman, before his death in 1831 he wrote a number of scholarly books that include his magisterial 1804 *Celtic Researches on the Origin, Traditions and Languages of the Ancient Britons* and his 1809 *The Mythology and Rites of the British Druids.*

Going back in time, the death knell of the native Britons was sounded when Germanic tribes invaded and settled in the south and east of the island of Britain from about the early fifth century.

Known as the Anglo-Saxons, they were composed of the Jutes, from the area of the Jutland Peninsula in modern Denmark, the Saxons from Lower Saxony, in modern Germany and the Angles from the Angeln area of Germany.

It was the Angles who gave the name 'Engla land', or 'Aengla land' – better known as 'England.'

They held sway in what became England from approximately 550 until 1066, with the main kingdoms those of Sussex, Wessex, Northumbria, Mercia, Kent, East Anglia and Essex.

It was only in Cornwall, Wales, parts of the north of England and eastern Galloway in Scotland where the Brythonic culture retained a tenacious foothold – with these indigenous Britons referring to the Anglo-Saxons as 'Saeson' or 'Saxones.'

It is from this that the Scottish Gaelic term for 'English people' of 'Sasannach' derives, the Irish Gaelic 'Sasanach' and the Welsh 'Saeson.'

The first serious shock to Anglo-Saxon control of England came in 789 in the form of sinister black-sailed Viking ships that appeared over the horizon off the island monastery of Lindisfarne, in the northeast of the country.

Lindisfarne was sacked in an orgy of violence and plunder, setting the scene for what would be many more terrifying raids on the coastline of not only England, but also Ireland and Scotland.

But the Vikings, or 'Northmen', in common with the Anglo-Saxons of earlier times, were raiders who eventually stayed – establishing, for example, what became Jorvik, or York, and the trading port of Dublin, in Ireland.

Through intermarriage, the bloodlines of the Anglo-Saxons and the indigenous Britons such as those who would come to bear the Davies name also became infused with that of the Vikings.

But there would be another infusion of the blood of the 'Northmen' in the wake of the Norman

Conquest of 1066 – a key event in English history that ended Anglo-Saxon supremacy.

By 1066, England had become a nation with several powerful competitors to the throne.

In what were extremely complex family, political and military machinations, the English monarch was Harold II, who had succeeded to the throne following the death of Edward the Confessor.

But his right to the throne was contested by two powerful competitors – his brother-in-law King Harold Hardrada of Norway, in alliance with Tostig, Harold II's brother, and Duke William II of Normandy.

In what has become known as The Year of Three Battles, Hardrada invaded England and gained victory over the English king on September 20 at the battle of Fulford, in Yorkshire.

Five days later, however, Harold II decisively defeated his brother-in-law and brother at the battle of Stamford Bridge.

But he had little time to celebrate his victory, having to immediately march south from Yorkshire to encounter a mighty invasion force led by Duke William of Normandy that had landed at Hastings, in East Sussex.

Harold's battle-hardened but exhausted force confronted the Normans on October 14 in a battle subsequently depicted on the Bayeux Tapestry – a 23ft. long strip of embroidered linen thought to have been commissioned eleven years after the event by the Norman Odo of Bayeux.

Harold drew up a strong defensive position at the top of Senlac Hill, building a shield wall to repel Duke William's cavalry and infantry.

The Normans suffered heavy losses, but through a combination of the deadly skill of their archers and the ferocious determination of their cavalry they eventually won the day.

Anglo-Saxon morale had collapsed on the battlefield as word spread through the ranks that Harold had been killed – the Bayeux Tapestry depicting this as having happened when the English king was struck by an arrow to the head.

Amidst the carnage of the battlefield, it was difficult to identify Harold – the last of the Anglo-Saxon kings.

Some sources assert William ordered his body to be thrown into the sea, while others state it was secretly buried at Waltham Abbey.

What is known with certainty, however, is

that William in celebration of his great victory founded Battle Abbey, near the site of the battle, ordering
that the altar be sited on the spot where Harold was
believed to have fallen.

William was declared King of England on
December 25, and the complete subjugation of newly
conquered subjects followed.

Within an astonishingly short space of time,
Norman manners, customs and law were imposed on
England – laying the basis for what subsequently
became established 'English' custom and practice.

But beneath the surface, both old Anglo-
Saxon and Brythonic culture was not totally
eradicated.

Some aspects were absorbed into those of the
Normans, while faint echoes of the Brythonic past is
still seen today in the form of popular surnames such
as Davies.

Chapter three:

Battle honours

The Davies name is first found in Flintshire, while many of its bearers have stamped a significant mark on the historical record.

In Wales, some of the name today can claim a descent from a royal prince.

This is through the late twelfth century Cynrig Efell, Lord of Eglwsegle, a twin son of Madog ap Maredudd, the last prince of the Welsh kingdom of Powys, and who died in 1160.

Of Madog – whose name is sometimes also rendered as 'Madoc' – the ancient Welsh annals relate how:

> *While Madog lived there was no man*
> *Dared ravage his fair borders*
> *Yet nought of all he held*
> *Esteemed he his save by God's might*

Another ancestor of those who would adopt the Davies surname from the forename of David was Dafydd ap Gruffyd – David, son of Gruffyd – the royal prince who was the last independent ruler of Wales.

It was in January of 1283, after England's ambitious Plantagenet king Edward I surrounded what then remained of independent Wales with a ring of steel in the form of a massive army, that Daffydd ap Gruffyd launched an armed resistance movement.

In the same mould as Scotland's great freedom fighter William Wallace, he achieved a number of daring successes before eventually being captured in May of that year.

On the orders of Edward, he was subjected to the brutal ordeal of being dragged through the streets of Shrewsbury attached to a horse's tail and then hanged, drawn and quartered.

Continuing a Davies tradition of resistance to arbitrary power and rule, David Davies, born in 1812 and known in Welsh as Dai'r Canwr – David the Singer – was the farm labourer, lay preacher and poet who was sentenced to transportation to Van Diemen's Land, now modern-day Tasmania, for his part in the Rebecca Riots.

Taking place between 1839 and 1843 in South and Mid Wales, these riots involved farmers and other agricultural workers protesting over what they perceived as unjust taxation.

Often dressed as women to hide their identities

– hence the term 'Rebecca' Riots – they carried out attacks on toll-booths and turnpikes.

In December of 1843, Davies was tried and convicted for his part in demolishing a turnpike at Spudder's Bridge, near Kidwelly.

Pardoned in October of 1854, he returned from Van Diemen's Land to his native Wales, where he died in a fire in 1874; there is a statue to him outside the Barry Dock Offices in Barry, Vale of Glamorgan.

On rather more conventional fields of conflict, no fewer than three bearers of the proud name of Davies were recipients during the First World War of the Victoria Cross (VC), the highest award for valour in the face of enemy action for British and Commonwealth forces.

Born in 1886 in the Ogmore Vale, Glamorgan, James Davies had been a corporal in the 13th Battalion, The Royal Welch Fusiliers when, in July of 1917 at Polygon Wood, Pilkem, in Belgium, he performed the actions for which he was posthumously awarded the honour.

During an assault on the enemy's line, he single-handedly attacked a machine-gun emplacement and overcame its crew. Although wounded, he then led a bombing party on a successful assault on another enemy position.

He died later from wounds received, while his VC is now on display at the Royal Welch Fusiliers Museum, Caernarfon Castle.

Born in 1895 in Birkenhead, Cheshire, John Davies was a corporal in the 11th (Service) Battalion, South Lancashire Regiment.

In March of 1918 near Eppeville, France, he mounted a parapet in full view of the enemy and unleashed a storm of machine-gun fire that allowed his comrades to successfully withdraw to another position.

Taken prisoner after the action, he went on to serve in the Home Guard during the Second World War; he died in 1955, while his VC is now on display at the Imperial War Museum, London.

Both a fighter pilot and a Royal Navy officer, Richard Bell Davies won his VC after carrying out what is considered to have been the first ever combat search and rescue by aircraft.

Born in 1886 in Kensington, London, he was a Squadron Commander in 3 Squadron, Royal Naval Air Service, when in November of 1915 he carried out the action for which he was awarded the honour.

This was when, at Ferrijik Junction, in

Bulgaria, he managed against all the odds to land his aircraft in enemy territory and take-off again with a fellow pilot who had crash landed.

Later promoted to the rank of Vice-Admiral, he died in 1966, while his VC is now on display at the Fleet Air Arm Museum in Yeovil, Somerset.

Born in 1913 in Bernardsville, New Jersey, James Davies, better known as Jimmy Davies, was the first American-born airman to be killed in action during the Second World War.

Having moved with his family to their original homeland of Wales before the outbreak of the war in 1939, he joined the Royal Air Force.

Flying the Hawker Hurricane fighter with 79 Squadron, based at RAF Biggin Hill, he was shot down and killed in June of 1940 while on a mission over the French port of St Valery.

His death came on the same day he was due to be presented by King George V with the Distinguished Flying Cross (DFC) for having previously shot down six German aircraft.

In the world of politics, David John Denzil Davies, better known as Denzil Davies, is the British former Labour Party politician born in 1938 in Cynwyl Elfed, Carmarthenshire.

Qualifying as a barrister, he later served for 35 years as Member of Parliament (MP) for Llanelli, while he served as a Treasury Minister in the late 1970s in the government of Prime Minister James Callaghan.

Born in 1939, Bryan Davies is the British Labour Party politician who was elevated to the Peerage of the United Kingdom as Baron Davies of Oldham, of Broxbourne in the County of Herefordshire, in 1997.

Serving as Secretary to the Parliamentary Labour Party and Shadow Cabinet from 1979 until 1992, he also served from 1977 to 1979 as a member of the Medical Research Council.

Not only a Liberal Party politician but also a prominent nineteenth century Welsh entrepreneur, David Davies was born in 1818 in Llandinam, Montgomeryshire.

Mainly self-taught, he went on to become a coal magnate and was responsible for much of the industrialisation of the Rhondda Valley.

Liberal MP for Cardigan Boroughs from 1874 to 1885 and later for Cardiganshire and also responsible for building the first iron bridge in Montgomeryshire, he died in 1890.

He was the grandfather of the politician and philanthropist David Davies, born in Llandinam in 1880.

Liberal MP for Montgomeryshire from 1906 to 1929 and a leading supporter of the League of Nations that was set up in the aftermath of the First World War, he was also the founder in 1932 of the New Commonwealth Society "for the promotion of international peace and order."

Created 1st Baron Davis, before his death in 1944 he endowed the Chair in International Politics at the University of Wales, Aberystwyth that is also home to the David Davies Memorial Institute of International Studies.

Chapter four:

On the world stage

One of the most popular entertainers of the early years of the twentieth century, David Ivor Davies, born in 1893 in Cardiff, was better known as Ivor Novello.

Taking the Novello surname from his mother's maiden name, the Welsh composer, singer and actor was aged only 21 when he achieved his first success as a songwriter with *Keep the Home Fires Burning*.

The song was enormously popular throughout the First World War, as was his 1917 stage show *Theodore & Co*.

Turning to acting in the 1920s, he appeared in two Alfred Hitchcock silent films, *The Lodger* and *Downhill*, while throughout the 1930s he staged a number of London West End musical productions that included his 1935 *Glamorous Night* and, from 1937, *The Dancing Years*.

He died in 1957 while a number of his songs, including *Waltz of My Heart*, *And Mother Came Too* and *Why Isn't It You?* were used in the 2001 film

Gosford Park, in which he was portrayed by the actor Jeremy Northman.

Established two years before his death, The Ivor Novello Awards for Songwriting are awarded annually by the British Society of Songwriters, Composers and Authors to British songwriters and composers and also outstanding international songwriters.

In contemporary music, the brothers **Ray** and **Dave Davies** were members of the British rock band The Kinks.

Born in 1947 in Fort's Green, Muswell Hill, London, guitarist Dave Davies formed the band in 1963 while his older brother Ray, born in 1944, joined shortly afterwards as the band's lead singer and songwriter.

The Kinks enjoyed great success with a string of hits that include *You Really Got Me*, *Waterloo Sunset*, *Lola*, *Sunny Afternoon*, *Autumn Almanac* and *Dedicated Follower of Fashion*.

They disbanded in 1996, while they are inductees of both the Rock and Roll Hall of Fame and the UK Music Hall of Fame; both brothers have also enjoyed successful solo careers.

From music to the stage, **Windsor Davies**,

born in 1930 in Canning Town, London but returning to Wales with his parents as a young boy, is the actor best known for his role from 1974 to 1981 of Battery Sergeant Major Williams in the television sitcom *It Ain't Half Hot Mum*.

Along with co-star Don Estelle, he enjoyed a hit single in 1975 with a semi-comic version of *Whispering Grass*, while other television credits include the 1981-1991 sitcom *Never the Twain*, co-starring with Donald Sinden.

Also known as the voice of Sergeant Major Zero in the *Terrahawks* children's television series, his big screen credits include the *Carry On* comedies *Carry on Behind* and *Carry On England*.

Of Scots and English roots, **Jeremy Davies** is the American film and television actor whose big screen roles include that of the interpreter Corporal Timothy E. Upham in the 1998 *Saving Private Ryan*.

Born in 1969 in Traverse City, Michigan, and known for his role of the physicist Daniel Faraday in the television series *Lost*, he is also the recipient of two Primetime Emmy Award nominations for Outstanding Actor in a Drama Series for his role in the series *Justified*.

Best known for his role of the dwarf Gimli in

the *Lord of the Rings* trilogy of films, **John Rhys-Davies** is the Welsh actor born in 1944 in Ammanford, Carmarthenshire.

At 6ft. 1in. in height and one of the tallest members of the *Lord of the Rings* cast, it was thanks to the marvels of modern camera technology that he was able to appear as of significantly less stature.

Other film credits include that of the Arab excavator Sallah in the *Indiana Jones* series of films, while he also appeared in the 1980 television mini-series *Shogun*.

Born in 1973 in Ballarat, Victoria, **Kimberley Davies** is the Australian actress best known for her role of Annalise Hartman in the television soap *Neighbours*; other television credits include *Pacific Palisades*, *Ally McBeal* and *Friends*.

Also on television, **Ashley Slanina-Davies**, born in 1989 in Standish, Greater Manchester is the English actress best known for her role of Amy Barnes in the teen soap *Hollyoaks*.

Born in 1937 in Brixton, London, Freddie Davies is the comedian and actor who, after beginning his career as an entertainer in a holiday camp, became better known as **Freddie "Parrot Face" Davies**.

Also an actor on television shows that include *Heartbeat*, *Casualty* and *Last of the Summer Wine*, his film credits include the 1995 *Funny Bones* and the 2004 *Harry Potter and the Prisoner of Azbakan*.

Born in 1966 in Loughton, Essex, **Alan Davies** is the English comedian, actor and writer who, after beginning his career in stand-up comedy in 1988, won *Time Out* magazine's Best Young Comic accolade three years later.

Also winner of the 1994 Edinburgh Festival Critics Award for Comedy, he starred from 1997 to 2004 in the television mystery series *Jonathan Creek*, while he is also a panellist on the television show *QI*.

Born in 1923 in Wallasey, Merseyside, Richard Davies is the British television presenter better known as **Dickie Davies**.

Presenter of *World of Sport* from 1968 to 1985 and also a snooker presenter for a time, on radio he hosted sports bulletins on Classic FM.

Behind the camera lens, Stephen Russell Davies is the prolific Welsh television screenwriter and producer better known as **Russell T Davies**.

Born in Swansea in 1963, he is noted for his

role from 2005 to 2010 in the popular *Doctor Who* series and its spin-off *Torchwood*.

His other award-winning works include the series *Queer as Folk*, *Casanova* and the 2001 *Bob and Rose*, which won him a Television Award for Writer of the Year.

Also behind the camera lens, **Andrew Davies**, born in Cardiff in 1936, is the screenwriter and author made a Fellow of BAFTA in 2002.

His big screen credits include the 2001 *Bridget Jones's Diary*, the 2004 *Bridget Jones: The Edge of Reason* and the 2011 *The Tailor of Panama*; television credits include the 1980 *To Serve Them All My Days*, the 2008 *Sense and Sensibility* and, from 2011, *South Riding*.

Bearers of the Davies name have also excelled in the highly competitive world of sport.

On the athletics track, **Lyn Davies**, nicknamed "Lyn the Leap", is the champion Welsh former long jumper born in 1942 in Nantymoel, near Bridgend; the recipient of a CBE, he won the gold medal in the event at the 1964 Olympics in Tokyo and also at the 1966 European Championships in Budapest.

In snooker, **Alex Davies**, born in 1987 Essex

became at the age of 16 the youngest person ever to win the English Amateur Championship.

In the rough and tumble that is the game of rugby, **Adrian Davies** is the Wales former international rugby union fly-half, born in Bridgend in 1969, who played for his nation in the 1991 and 1995 Rugby World Cup finals.

Nicknamed "Cowboy", Charles Lynn Davies, better known as **Lynn Davies**, is the Welsh former international rugby union prop born in 1929 in Bancyfelin.

Born in Ynysybwl in 1948, **Alan Davies** is the Welsh rugby union coach who coached the national team from 1991 to 1995.

From the rugby pitch to the football pitch, **Dai Davies**, born in Glanaman in 1948, is the former player who, in addition to playing for teams that include Swansea City, Everton and Wrexham, played for the Wales national team between 1975 and 1982.

In the swimming pool, **David Davies**, born in 1985 in Barry, won the gold medal in the 1500-metres freestyle event at the 2006 Commonwealth Games in Melbourne.

From sport to the written word, **Hunter**

Davies is the prolific author, journalist and broadcaster born in 1936 in Renfrewshire, Scotland, but who moved to Carlisle, in England, after living for a time in the Scottish town of Dumfries.

Renowned for his 1968 authorised biography of the Beatles, *The Beatles*, he is also the author of books that include the 1965 *Here We Go, Round the Mulberry Bush*, later adapted for the film of the name.

Married to the writer Margaret Forster, he has also written a biography of the late Lake District fell walker Alfred Wainwright in addition to ghost writing autobiographies of footballers Paul Gascoigne, Wayne Rooney and Dwight York.

Returning to the stage, **Rupert Davies**, born in 1916 and who died in 1976, was the British actor best known for playing the title role on television of the French detective *Maigret*, based on the novels of George Simenon.

It was under rather odd circumstances that he first honed his acting skills.

Serving in the Fleet Air Arm during the Second World War, he was captured and interned in a German prisoner-of-war camp after being shot down over the Dutch coast in 1940.

Taking part in theatre performances in the camp to provide entertainment for his fellow prisoners, he took up acting as a career following the end of the war – with early television credits that include *Quatermass II*, *Ivanhoe* and *Emergency – Ward 10* – but it was for his role of *Maigret* that he became famous.

Having released the single *Smoking My Pipe* that referred to the iconic opening sequence of *Maigret* where he lights his pipe and contentedly puffs away on it, in 1965 he became the first person to win the annual Pipe Smoker of the Year Award.